MongoDB and PHP

Steve Francia

O'REILLY®

Beijing · Cambridge · Farnham · Köln · Sebastopol · Tokyo

MongoDB and PHP
by Steve Francia

Published by O'Reilly Media, Inc., 1005 Gravenstein Highway North, Sebastopol, CA 95472.

O'Reilly books may be purchased for educational, business, or sales promotional use. Online editions
are also available for most titles (*http://my.safaribooksonline.com*). For more information, contact our
corporate/institutional sales department: (800) 998-9938 or *corporate@oreilly.com*.

Editors: Mike Loukides and Shawn Wallace	**Cover Designer:** Karen Montgomery
Production Editor: Jasmine Perez	**Interior Designer:** David Futato
Copyeditor: Chet Chin	**Illustrator:** Robert Romano
Proofreader: O'Reilly Production Services	

Revision History for the First Edition:
   2012-01-24   First release
See *http://oreilly.com/catalog/errata.csp?isbn=9781449314361* for release details.

ISBN: 978-1-449-31436-1

[LSI]

1327093091

Table of Contents

Preface

Once every decade or so, a technology comes along that is so revolutionary that it fundamentally alters the way we approach everything we do. The world itself has changed. As I think back to 1995 when I first started developing Internet applications, our data needs were relatively simple. For the next 10 years, little changed; more and more people were using the Internet, and consequently data stores needed to scale to larger workloads, but caching largely took care of that, as all users were accessing the same set of data. As social media came to fruition, it was clear that the approach that had worked for the prior 30 years was not longer sufficient. In the future, all data and experience would need to be personalized—on a large scale. It was out of this need that MongoDB was created. A database for today's applications, a database for today's challenges, a database for today's scale: MongoDB has that disruptive potential that will fundamentally change the way *you* approach developing applications.

I'd like to publicly thank my wife and four children for being patient with me as I spent most of my free time over the past few months writing this book.

Conventions Used in This Book

The following typographical conventions are used in this book:

Italic
Indicates new terms, URLs, email addresses, filenames, and file extensions.

`Constant width`
Used for program listings, as well as within paragraphs to refer to program elements such as variable or function names, databases, data types, environment variables, statements, and keywords.

`Constant width bold`
Shows commands or other text that should be typed literally by the user.

`Constant width italic`
Shows text that should be replaced with user-supplied values or by values determined by context.

This icon signifies a tip, suggestion, or general note.

 This icon indicates a warning or caution.

Using Code Examples

This book is here to help you get your job done. In general, you may use the code in this book in your programs and documentation. You do not need to contact us for permission unless you're reproducing a significant portion of the code. For example, writing a program that uses several chunks of code from this book does not require permission. Selling or distributing a CD-ROM of examples from O'Reilly books does require permission. Answering a question by citing this book and quoting example code does not require permission. Incorporating a significant amount of example code from this book into your product's documentation does require permission.

We appreciate, but do not require, attribution. An attribution usually includes the title, author, publisher, and ISBN. For example: "*MongoDB and PHP* by Steve Francia (O'Reilly). Copyright 2011 Steve Francia, 978-1-4493-1436-1."

If you feel your use of code examples falls outside fair use or the permission given above, feel free to contact us at *permissions@oreilly.com*.

Safari® Books Online

 Safari Books Online is an on-demand digital library that lets you easily search over 7,500 technology and creative reference books and videos to find the answers you need quickly.

With a subscription, you can read any page and watch any video from our library online. Read books on your cell phone and mobile devices. Access new titles before they are available for print, and get exclusive access to manuscripts in development and post feedback for the authors. Copy and paste code samples, organize your favorites, download chapters, bookmark key sections, create notes, print out pages, and benefit from tons of other time-saving features.

O'Reilly Media has uploaded this book to the Safari Books Online service. To have full digital access to this book and others on similar topics from O'Reilly and other publishers, sign up for free at *http://my.safaribooksonline.com*.

How to Contact Us

Please address comments and questions concerning this book to the publisher:

O'Reilly Media, Inc.
1005 Gravenstein Highway North
Sebastopol, CA 95472
800-998-9938 (in the United States or Canada)
707-829-0515 (international or local)
707-829-0104 (fax)

We have a web page for this book, where we list errata, examples, and any additional information. You can access this page at:

http://shop.oreilly.com/product/0636920022381.do

To comment or ask technical questions about this book, send email to:

bookquestions@oreilly.com

For more information about our books, courses, conferences, and news, see our website at *http://www.oreilly.com*.

Find us on Facebook: *http://facebook.com/oreilly*

Follow us on Twitter: *http://twitter.com/oreillymedia*

Watch us on YouTube: *http://www.youtube.com/oreillymedia*

CHAPTER 1

Why Mongo?

One of the problems that led to the first dot-com crash was the huge expense of development, especially server software. A new and viable set of open source tools emerged from the ashes of the first dot-com and became the foundation for the next generation of the Internet. In the summer of 2001, a new acronym emerged; LAMP—Linux, Apache, MySQL and PHP—became the platform of choice for an entire generation of developers. And like that, PHP and MySQL were married (they were right next to each other, after all). The two seemed destined to go together forever.

The Problem of Objects and Relational Data Structures

There was only one problem. PHP—which started as a templating language—matured and gradually embraced objects. PHP was being used in more complex applications and the language consistently changed to meet these ever-increasing demands. The practice of writing raw SQL queries in template files quickly became unacceptable (some say it was never acceptable). As the problems became more and more complex, tools were written to solve the constantly growing trouble of PHP using objects (or arrays) and MySQL (and the other relational databases) using tables, rows, and columns.

This isn't a problem specific to PHP. For decades, people have built tools and libraries to automate the process of translating objects to relational data structures. The most popular set is called Object Relational Mappers (ORMs). ORMs were built to solve the problem of SQL. Their sales pitch is: use an ORM because it masks all the nasty details of the datastore, so all you ever need to touch is your friendly PHP objects. Although tools emerged that did a reasonable job of making good on that promise, they never really worked perfectly. First, you always needed to remember that there was a relational database behind these objects that spoke in terms of tables, rows, and columns. Second, these ORMs came at a high cost. They added a lot of complexity and overhead to applications and persisted only a subset of SQLs features. As they developed, it quickly became the case that learning an ORM was far more time-consuming than learning SQL in the first place. It is sufficient to say that although the ORMs largely fixed the problems of SQL, they brought with them the problems of ORMs.

The Problem with ORMs

The objective of an ORM may be simple, but the solution never is.

ORMs Are Hairy and Complex

Propel and Doctrine are the two most popular ORMs for PHP. Propel follows an active record model; Doctrine follows hibernate. Both projects are quite large, comprising tens of thousands of lines of code. Doctrine also provides its own SQL-like query language called DQL, so you need to know both SQL and DQL to use Doctrine.

ORMs Aren't Performant

The core objective of the ORM is developer convenience. The core objective of an ORM is developer convenience as they are built to translate the database's tables, rows, and columns into your languages objects. The most common approach is called Active Record. It is especially easy to use but carries with it some of the worst performance compromises to do so. This is universally true, but especially in PHP. Typically they perform reasonably well with low activity, but as load or data size increases, their performance compromises become a large hindrance. A common criticism is that Ruby on Rails doesn't scale, and it's best as a prototype environment. This is an accurate criticism, but it is important to recognize that the place that it doesn't scale isn't the controller or view, it's the Active Record layer. Not only do ORMs add a layer of overhead at runtime, but they also consume a lot of memory.

ORMs Neutered SQL

It wasn't just that the ORMs made it so that SQL was hidden; they stripped it down to its most basic features. ORMs made it really quite simple to do the operational stuff like reading and writing objects, commonly called CRUD (Create Read Update Delete) operations, but failed in large part to support any of SQL's advanced features. If you don't believe me, try to do a left outer join with an ORM or an aggregate function like an average across a set of data. Many have even failed to provide support for database transactions, passing along the responsibility to the application.

Complicated Architecture

In an effort to address some of the performance shortcomings of ORMs and relational databases in general, MemCache was built. MemCache was so effective at speeding up data retrieval that it was quickly adopted across the industry. It soon became a necessary element for any application looking to scale or even just perform acceptably. In fact, it may have had the highest percentage of adoption of a single technology, nearly every website or application on the internet uses it.

While MemCache works well to quickly access data, it does little to simplify our applications. With the addition of MemCache, ORMs or applications have to not only manage translating objects to tables, rows, and columns, but also the additional logic to store these objects behind a key (or set of keys) and track when to retrieve data from MemCache versus the RDBMS and when to expire the data in MemCache to ensure that the RDBMS and MemCache data are in sync—not a trivial task and one that often concludes in a "good enough" state, leaving undesirable results.

PHP Is Mostly CRUD

With all the problems with ORMs, you may wonder why programmers use them at all. People were willing to make the compromises to adopt ORMs for one big reason; PHP applications are by and large CRUD applications. Rarely do they use all of the rich features the relational database provides, so giving them up seemed a small price to pay for the benefit of simplified access to the data. Additionally, there weren't really any other good options. For very simple projects, one could write SQL in one's code, but this was hard to debug and even harder to ensure that it was done securely. PHP is famous for enabling SQL injection attacks, as inexperienced developers pass variables right into the SQL without sanitization.

MongoDB, Optimized for Operation

Ever wonder what would happen if someone optimized a data store for the type of operations application developers actually use?

In 2007, two brilliant developers, Eliot Horowitz and Dwight Merriman (the founders of 10gen), set out to do just that. Both had previously worked at DoubleClick—Dwight as CTO and founder and Eliot as an engineer—designing the system that served and tracked hundreds of thousands of ads per second and were intimately familiar with the challenges of building a high-volume, high-transaction, scaleable system with existing database technologies. They knew the challenges well and what current relational database offerings lacked. They set out to build a database optimized for operations and scale. They called their database MongoDB.

The driving philosophy behind MongoDB was to retain as much functionality as possible while permitting horizontal scale and, at the same time, to ensure that the developer experience is as elegant as possible.

As they set out to build MongoDB, they looked at the features provided by relational databases and asked what we could live without and still make it easy for the developer to work with. Relationships make horizontal scale impossible and multiple table transactions hard to do on distributed clusters. They then looked at improving the developer experience. Key value stores are great, but often more functionality is needed. Sometimes we need to access things by something other than the key. Since most languages today operate on objects, what if MongoDB used a data structure that resembled an object?

MongoDB Is a Document Database

The founders decided to build MongoDB as a document database. At the highest level of organization, it is quite similar to a relational database, but as you get closer to the data itself, you will notice a significant change in the way the data is stored. Instead of databases, tables, columns, and rows you have databases, collections, and documents (see Figure 1-1).

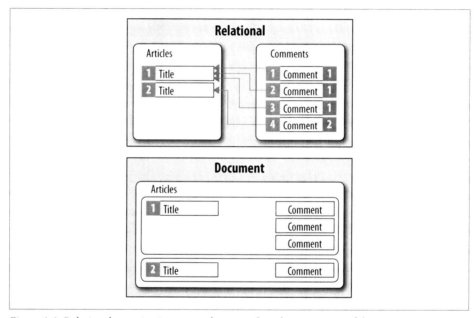

Figure 1-1. Relational organization versus document-based organization of data

Document == Array

Often people think of PDF files and Word documents when they hear the term "document database," which isn't accurate. For all intents and purposes, a document is equivalent to an array in PHP.

Databases

MongoDB groups data into databases in the very same way as most relational databases do. If you have any experience with relational databases, you should think of these the same way. In an RDBMS, a database is a set of tables, stored procedures, views, and so on. In MongoDB, a database is a set of collections.

Collections

Collections correlate to tables within the relational database paradigm. For most purposes, you can think of them as tables (just don't call them that). Just like tables, indexes are applied to collections. A collection is a collection of documents and indexes.

Documents

In MongoDB, the primary object is called a document. A document doesn't have a direct correlation in the relational world. Documents do not have a predefined schema like relational database tables. A document is partly a row, in that it's where the data is located, but it's also part columns, in that the schema is defined in each document (not table-wide).

The best way to think of a document is as a multidimensional array. In an array, you have a set of keys that map to values. The values could themselves be another array. In practical matters, a MongoDB document is a JSON array. Documents map extremely well to objects and other PHP data types like arrays and even multidimensional arrays.

As this text is intended for a PHP audience, the PHP array has the closest correlation of any data type. It's nearly a perfect 1-to-1 correlation. It's important to note that the PHP arrays are unique, as they permit key ⇒ value as well as enumerated keys. Not only can both types be used as an array, but they can coexist in the same array. Additionally, PHP doesn't have the ability to have unordered arrays. MongoDB uses JSON for its data store, which doesn't share these same properties. In a JavaScript JSON representation, there is a difference between a list (which has unordered, unkeyed values) and a hash (key/value pairs). In practical use, however, this difference is rarely, if ever, noticed.

MongoDB Is Optimized for CRUD Operations

MongoDB wasn't written in a lab. It was written to solve real-world problems. It has been optimized to be extremely efficient at operational procedures. Great care was taken to optimize it in a few ways. The first thing you should notice in using MongoDB is that documents are really powerful. You can store a lot of associated data in a single document while keeping your data structured, normalized, and able to be queried. Whereas you previously needed to access a dozen or more tables to retrieve data for a given object, often in MongoDB this can be accomplished in a single document. Most CRUD operations become very simple save, find, and delete operations.

Optimal Interface for Developers

Because a MongoDB document is effectively a PHP object or array, creating a new document is easy. All you need to do is create a new PHP array or object and save it. The majority of this book will explain the various ways to interact with MongoDB from PHP. While it may require an adjustment from the relational way of thinking (which so many developers are accustomed to), the interface to MongoDB is a pleasure to use and feels very natural. By and large, things work in the way you would expect them to and in a way that will make you a more efficient developer.

Optimal Performance

MongoDB was designed from the ground up to be a very high-performance database. By itself, MongoDB provides measurable performance increases over relational data-bases on similar operations; however, many applications will experience a considerable improvement in performance (20x or more isn't uncommon). This is because the core database operations are not only faster but also much more straightforward. For instance, inserting a blog post into a relational database may require inserts into many tables, such as a post table, a few inserts into a tags table, a few inserts into a posts_to_tags table, insert into a category table, inserts into a media table and corre-sponding joining table—the list could go on. This same overall objective can be accomplished with a single document write in MongoDB.

In addition to simplier and faster operations, MongoDB also makes heavy use of mem-ory mapped files. At the risk of oversimplifying things, essentially what this means is that MongoDB performs read-through, write-through memory caching on all working data (or as much as will fit into RAM). With MongoDB, there really isn't a need for MemCache for most use cases.

Optimal Simplicity

Even with very complex structured data, MongoDB is fully optimized for creating, reading, updating, and deleting objects. As described in the previous section, many operations that previously required complex joins or multitable transactions can usu-ally be accomplished with a much simpler schema, which results in simpler operations and a significantly more straightforward model layer. Additionally, without the need to maintain cache and worrying about updating and expiring data, not only is the application simplified, but so is the architecture.

The Value of Consistency

MongoDB is a *fully consistent* database in the same tradition as MySQL, PostgreSQL and most of the relational databases. This is one differentiator between MongoDB and the majority of the databases in the NoSQL space which are eventually consistent. Some eventually consistent databases, also called multi master databases, make claims to have full consistency, but such claims fall short as they require a redefinition of the term "consistency."

While there is certainly a place for eventually consistent databases, most developers don't realize what functionality they are giving up when they accept this compromise. It's not just about data loss, but about functionality. With fully consistent databases, you can do things like increment values easily or append items without worrying about collisions. While these operations are trivial to perform in MongoDB, such operations in eventually consistent databases are impossible without a ton of extra logic and handling in the application.

To illustrate this difference, I'll use a simple example. Say you wanted to write a very simple voting application that tracked the username of each voter (each user can only vote once) and the total. The logic is pretty straightforward: if a username is not in the array, increment the total and append the username to the array. In MongoDB, this is a very straightforward (and atomic) operation, but it's impossible to do with an eventually consistent database.

CHAPTER 2

PHP, MongoDB, and You

This chapter will provide the foundational knowledge of working with MongoDB and PHP. By the end of the chapter, you can expect to be able to install the driver and build an application in PHP that uses MongoDB as the data store.

Installing the Driver on Linux or MacOS X

As distributions and environments vary, installation instructions will also vary. It's important to have a basic understanding of your operating system or distribution, particularly as it pertains to PHP. Hopefully, these general instructions will provide enough information for you to be able to customize them for your particular situation.

Checking for the Driver

Before you install the driver, you should first check to see if the driver is already present. A growing number of distributions include the MongoDB driver as part of the base install. The following command will return a bunch of information about the driver if it is installed:

```
php --re mongo
```

If you do not have the extension installed, you will see:

```
Exception: Extension mongo does not exist
```

Installing the Driver

There are a few different ways to install the PHP MongoDB driver. If you are using Zend Server, you are already good to go. The Zend Server ships with the MongoDB driver already installed. Some distributions maintain their own deb or rpm packages to install the driver, and while this approach works, it is not the recommended approach. It's recommended to use PECL to install the driver, as it's consistent across all systems, provides an easy upgrade path, and is kept up to date.

Obviously, this approach depends on PECL installed and configured properly. It is beyond the scope of this text; many distributions include it, but in the event that you get "command not found," there are many online guides to installing PECL for your given OS. Depending on your OS and configuration, you may need to "sudo pecl" for each command.

The PHP MongoDB client extension can be installed using the following PECL command:

```
pecl install mongo
```

If everything works properly, you'll see:

```
Build process completed successfully
Installing '/usr/lib/php/modules/mongo.so'
install ok: channel://pecl.php.net/mongo-1.0.4
You should add "extension=mongo.so" to php.ini
```

Add the following line to your *php.ini* configuration and you're good to go:

```
extension=mongo.so" to php.ini
```

Upgrading the Driver

Upgrading the driver is a bit trickier, as it's fairly important for system consistency to use the same upgrade approach as was used to install the driver. As stated earlier, PECL is the preferred installation method. With PECL, it's as simple as:

```
pecl update-channels
pecl upgrade mongo
```

You will need to restart your web server to reload the new extension.

Installing the Driver on Windows

MongoDB has full support for Windows and is one of the few NoSQL solutions to do so. Pecl runs fine on Windows, so feel free to try that approach if you have pecl installed and configured. As an alternative, the MongoDB project distributes a precompiled version of the driver for windows. You can download this from github at *https://github .com/mongodb/mongo-php-driver/downloads*. Make sure to put the correct dll (thread safe or regular) into the folder where all of your other php plugins are located, then add the appropriate line to the extensions section of your *php.ini* file.

While there are many ways to install AMP (Apache MySQL/MongoDB PHP) for Windows, one approach I like to use is the Uniform Server. It's an all-in-one solution that doesn't require much heavy lifting or configuration. In most cases, you just unpack and run it. The Uniform Server 6 has a MongoDB plugin, which provides the MongoDB server, the MongoDB PHP driver, and a simple browser-based admin called phpMoAdmin. Uniform Server also provides a Windows interface to start, stop, and administer the various services. More information on Uniform Server can be found through its website, *http://www.uniformserver.com.*

Connecting to a Database

This text assumes you already have MongoDB installed and accessible. It is beyond the scope of this text to instruct you in installation. Many great resources already exist to do so. I'll recommend the MongoDB documentation, which is always kept up to date at *http://mongodb.org.*

Connecting to a MongoDB Database Server

Connecting to MongoDB from PHP is very similar to connecting to any other database. The default host is `localhost`, and the default port is `27017`. If using the defaults, both (or either) can be omitted from the connection string.

Connecting to MongoDB database server at localhost port 27017:

```
$connection = new Mongo();
```

Connecting to a remote host with optional custom port:

```
$connection = new Mongo( "172.20.10.8:65018" );
```

Selecting a Database

Once the database server connection is established, we will use it to access a database. The defined way to do this is:

```
$db = $connection->selectDB('dbname');
```

As is often the case, there is more than one way accomplish the same thing. As with many other operations in MongoDB, there is a shorthand way to selecting a database:

```
$db = $connection->dbname;
```

 Mongo will not throw an error if you try to select a database that doesn't exist but will instead create a new database with that name. This makes it extra critical to double-check your names. If you ever connect to a database and wonder where your data went, the first thing to do is make sure you didn't accidentally mistype the name and inadvertently create a new (empty) database.

The Basics (CRUD Operations)

Because the majority of your database interactions focus on creating, manipulating, and finding data, this section will focus on the fundamental Create, Read, Update, and

Delete—better known as CRUD—operations as well as how to find and retrieve this data.

Creating/Selecting a Collection

Now that we have created and connected to a database, let's do something with it. The first thing we need to do is create a collection. Selecting (and creating) a collection is very similar to accessing and creating a database. We will use the database handle we already created in the previous section:

```
$collection = $db->addresses;
```

Alternatively, we can connect to the database and select a collection in a single step:

```
$addresses = $connection->dbname->addresses;
```

Up to this point, everything has happened pretty much the same way as if you were connecting to a relational database, but it is important to pay attention to what we haven't done. We haven't typed any "CREATE DATABASE" commands. We haven't created any tables or collections. We haven't defined any schemas. All we have done is access the database through the PHP interface as provided by the MongoDB driver and MongoDB has done all of this for us.

Creating a Document

Creating a document in MongoDB couldn't be easier. Create an array. Pass it into the insert method on the collection object.

```
$address = array(
    'first_name' => 'Peter',
    'last_name'  => 'Parker',
    'address'    => '175 Fifth Ave',
    'city'       => 'New York',
    'state'      => 'NY',
    'zip'        => '10010'
    );

$addresses->insert($address);
```

Alternatively, we could use the save method. The save method works just like the insert method, except that if an _id value is specified and exists, save will update instead of insert the array. In practice, I nearly always use save as it leads to much more reusable code in most circumstances.

Important Details about Updating

MongoDB's typical operation is *asynchronous*. This means that when you insert a record, it will not return a value. This is often referred to as "fire and forget it" operation. It provides a number of advantages when writing data, which is typically a more expensive operation. Rather than blocking the running of the PHP script until the database completes the request and returns, with MongoDB the script will not block on this operation and will process much faster. To be clear, this behavior doesn't provide better database performance, but rather better application performance, especially under heavy load.

MongoDB can also insert *synchronously*. This will also hold execution of the PHP script until it has finished inserting. This is similar to how MySQL, PostgreSQL and other databases work. In this behavior, the application must wait for the database. Under heavy load, this can cause all sorts of issues as connections stack up waiting for processes to finish (just like the relational databases), so it's important to use the default unless you have a good reason for doing otherwise.

The methods `update`, `insert`, `remove`, and `save all` accept an additional parameter, which is an array of options.

To perform synchronous operations, pass the "safe" option and set it to true in the options array:

```
$addresses->insert($address, array('safe' => true));
```

The `insert` method itself will add the about-to-be-created `_id` to the array (or object) passed in. This behavior is important to understand and likely represents a change from what you are likely used to. It does this before sending the data over to the database. The `insert` method does not return the primary key; rather, it sets it on the array or object provided. To access the primary key, simply reference it:

```
$pk = $address['_id'];
```

When the safe parameter is passed in, the program will wait for the database response. If the update doesn't succeed, the cursor will throw a `MongoCursorException`. Alternatively, one can also set `safe` to an integer. In a replicated system, this will ensure that that number of systems receives the data before returning successfully. If it is unable to perform the operation on the number of specified nodes, it will throw a `MongoCursorTimeoutException` after it times out. One should be careful when using this feature to not set the number too high; for instance, if one set it to 3 for a three-node cluster, it would work fine unless a node went down. Then it would cease to perform updates while hanging the application for a long time on each operation. `timeout` is another parameter that can be passed in the options array and will define the number of milliseconds before throwing a timeout exception.

About Consistency

A common misconception is that "safe" means consistent. MongoDB is a fully consistent system, unlike multimaster systems (dynamo), which are eventually consistent. This means that any time you read from a master, you will always get the same data. In a multimaster system, it's possible to retrieve a record from two different masters and get back two different versions of that same record. One may want to use the synchronous behavior if writing to a collection with an index enforcing uniqueness.

Then the application can ensure that the write happened and handle the case if the write was denied because of an existing value.

About fsync

Another available option is `fsync`, which forces a write to disk (and also implies "safe"). One of the write performance optimizations MongoDB uses is that it pools writes and flushes them to the disk every so often rather than constantly writing. Prior to MongoDB 1.8, the `fsync` option was the only way to ensure that the changes weren't vulnerable to being lost in the event of a failure (kernel panic, hardware failure, etc.) occuring between the time the change was accepted and when it was actually written to disk. From version 1.8 on, MongoDB has included a write-ahead journal, which ensures that data loss doesn't occur. With journaling enabled, there isn't really a need for `fsync`, and it shouldn't be used.

Primary Keys and ObjectIds

MongoDB uses primary keys, just like most other databases. Primary keys need to be unique. Unless otherwise configured, MongoDB will automatically create a primary key for each document. In MongoDB, these are called ObjectIds. *ObjectIds in MongoDB are not strings or integers, but objects.* This is very important, as you will see in a minute as we try to query for this document.

The ObjectId is composed of a timestamp, as well as information about the machine it was created on. As an object, it has methods that you can run. The most helpful is likely the `getTimestamp` method, which will return the timestamp:

```
$id->getTimestamp();
```

About Primary Keys

While MongoDB will provide a `uniqueId` for the document if one doesn't exist, it will also readily accept one provided to it. Simply set the `_id` element of the array to an ObjectId, int, string, or other. This is especially useful when using a collection that is often referenced and contains an immutable key—for example, a username that would be referenced and displayed by various other objects but isn't changable (depending on your application and business rules). Objects that already have a naturally occuring unique identifier should be considered in place of an ObjectId. Doing so would save not only additional space but also the overhead of another index.

It is important to note that an array can't be used as the primary key.

Reading a Document

MongoDB doesn't use a structured query language (SQL) or any kind of query language; rather, you provide an array of what you would like returned. It retains the flexibility in large part of SQL but is in most cases much simpler.

Like a key value store, you can access the document by the primary key:

```
$id = new MongoId('4ba667b0a90578631c9caea1');
$pp = $addresses->findone( array( '_id' => $id ) );
```

Unlike a key value store, you can access the document by any other key:

```
$pp = $addresses->findone( array(
    'first_name' => 'Peter',
    'last_name' => 'Parker'
    ) );
```

As you can see, it is very straightforward to access documents from MongoDB. It's important to note here that this is without the benefit of any external libraries other than the driver.

This doesn't require a pre-existing index (though like any query it would benefit from one). This is an important distinction as many other NoSQL solutions claim to have the ability to perform secondary indexes, but not ad hoc queries like the query above, but require a separate index to be previously established and maintained.

About ObjectIds

It nearly goes without saying that it is important that the primary key matches what you are querying for. If you provide a string and it is expecting an object, it won't match. So if your primary key is `ObjectId("4ba667b0a90578631c9caea1")`, this is not the same as the string `"4ba667b0a90578631c9caea1"`. This is a common mistake of new MongoDB users. As you are free to use any primary key you want, you could use a UUID or other string, but there are advantages to using an ObjectId. One advantage is that unlike UUIDs, ObjectIds have a predefined order to them and won't require loading the index on insert. Another advantage is that because the ObjectId also contains a timestamp, you can avoid a `created_at` field in most cases. Additionally, the ObjectId is 12 bytes, whereas a UUID is 16 bytes.

Retrieving Select Values

By default, MongoDB will return the entire document (or set of documents) rather than a set of values. The find and findone methods accept a second parameter that is an array of the fields to return:

```
$pw = $db->users->findOne(array('username' => 'spf13'), array('password'));
print($pw);
```

Updating a Document

Updating a document is just as straightforward. The `update` method takes two parameters. The second is what to do (action) and the first is what to do it to (criteria). There is also a third optional parameter whereby you can pass in an array of options.

Updates in MongoDB are quite performant for the most part. MongoDB takes advantage of memory mapped files and buffers actually writing to disk. Additionally, MongoDB does `in place` updates on disk, provided that there is room. By default, MongoDB pads each document a small amount so that updates of a similar size can do `in place` writes.

Changing a Value

Use `update` to change a value:

```
$addresses->update(
    array( '_id' => new MongoId('4ba667b0a90578631c9caea1')),
    array( '$set' => array( 'zip' => '10011' ) )
);
```

There are a few things to take note of here. Your first instinct may have been to simply pass in the array containing the `new key` ⇒ `value` into the second parameter. You can certainly do that, but MongoDB will interpret that as you wanting to replace the entire document with the provided array. Not what we want to do here.

To avoid this behavior, we use an operator. In this example, are using `$set`, which does exactly what we want, only setting (either adding or changing) the value specified and leaving the remainder of the document intact.

As an alternative approach, we could have read the document into PHP, modified the array, and provided the entire array in the second parameter. As a standalone operation, this would have had the same end result, but with a few potentially negative side effects. First, the `in place` updates are slightly more efficient. Second, the `in place` operators (like `$set`) are atomic. What if two different users read the same document into PHP at the same time, modified it in PHP and then performed a save operation and passed in the new array? A simple example might be that while you are editing a blog post, another user adds a comment to that post that is stored in the same document. Whichever document is written last will overwrite the first even if the first changed different keys from the second. In this example, the comment would mysteriously disappear. The `in place` operators prevent this often undesirable behavior.

Up to this point, we haven't done anything we couldn't have done in a relational database. For the next example, we will add a nested array to our document.

Adding a Value

Use update to add a value:

```
$addresses->update(
    array( 'first_name' => 'Peter', 'last_name' => 'Parker'),
    array( '$set' =>
        array( 'superpowers' =>
            array( 'agility', 'stamina', 'spidey sense', 'web shooters',
                    'super human strength', 'super human intelligence' )
        )
    )
);
```

We have just added a new value to the document using the same $set operator in the previous example. We did this all without modifying any tables, and without using any join tables. The new value is in itself another array, which is transparently stored as part of the same document.

Appending a Value to an Array

Another example of using an in place operator. A unique property of MongoDB is that an array is a native data type. One of the neat things you can do is append values atomically to an array:

```
$addresses->update(
    array( 'first_name' => 'Peter', 'last_name' => 'Parker'),
    array( '$push' => array( 'superpowers' => 'wall crawling' ))
);
```

This example is especially important that the operator is atomic. If you didn't take this approach and multiple comments were appended to a blog post by reading in the post document and manually adding another comment onto the list, then saving it, you would lose comments. An advantage of using a fully consistent database is the ability to have these atomic operations that facilitate such operations.

One thing to pay attention to when appending values is that if frequently done on the same document, the updates will require more space than allocated on disk for that document, causing MongoDB to find a new spot on disk for that document. Done too frequently, this causes a lot of thrashing on disk and can hinder performance (every once in a while is fine). An example of such bad behavior would be a logging application that appends a new value to the document every minute. A much better approach would be to prepopulate the expected fields. For example, in this logging application, one would initially create a document with all 1,440 keys set to a placeholder like "0", then every minute update the key for that minute rather than appending it. It's a fairly specific case, but an important one to point out—and one we encounter a lot.

A note on terminology

Nested arrays such as we have just created are called by a variety of names: embedded document, nested array, nested hash, embedded hash, dictionary, and so on. This can be confusing, just remember that they are all the same thing.

Upsert and Multiple

Two of the options are worthy of note here.

Upsert changes the behavior so that if the criteria provided doesn't exist, it will create a new document with that criteria.

Multiple enables the method to update more than one document.

These two options are exclusive. There is no way upsert multiple documents.

Saving a Document

What's the difference between update, insert, and save?

Save is simply a wrapper for insert and update. If an _id is provided, it will update; otherwise, it will insert. You can safely use save pretty much all the time, unless you want to be very explicit as to which of the two operations you are performing.

For the sake of example, as well as providing data to query against later, we will add another record using save. This time, we will pass an object instead of an array to show the versatility of the save method. The methods save, insert, and update all accept objects or arrays as the data parameter:

```
class Hero {}

$hero = new Hero();

$hero->first_name = 'Eliot';
$hero->last_name = 'Horowitz';
$hero->address = '134 Fifth Ave';
$hero->city = 'New York';
$hero->state = 'NY';
$hero->zip = '10010';
$hero->superpowers = array( 'agility', 'super human intelligence', 'wall crawling' );

$addresses->save($hero);
```

Deleting a Document

Deleting is as straightforward as adding and updating and follows the same pattern as updating:

```
$criteria = array('_id'=> new MongoId('4ba667b0a90578631c9caea1'));
$addresses->remove($criteria, array("justOne" => true) );
```

 Unlike update, the remove method by default will remove all documents matching the provided criteria. There is an additional optional parameter, which is an array of options. One of these is justOne, which would limit the deletion to a single document. As a best practice, justOne should be used wherever it is applicable.

The MongoDB Shell

This is probably as good a time as any to introduce the MongoDB Shell. Although you certainly could develop a successful application without using it, you should be aware of it as you will likely find good reasons to use it. The MongoDB Shell is a JavaScript-based tool for administering the database and accessing and manipulating data. It is similar to the PHP (or other language) driver, with the following primary differences:

1. It's a shell, so it works in a synchronous fashion (in other words, all methods are run in "safe" mode).
2. The interface is JavaScript.
3. It can issue administrative commands.

mongo

On the command line, type:

```
mongo
```

or, on Windows:

```
mongo.exe
```

This will automatically connect to a database (default to localhost port 27017). Once it loads, you select the database you want to access and you can run queries.

Using the Shell

Following the same commands as the previous section, only this time in the shell:

```
> use dbname
> db.addresses.insert({ "first_name" : "Peter",
                        "last_name" : "Parker",
                        "address" : "175 Fifth Ave",
                        "city" : "New York",
```

```
                      "state" : "NY",
                      "zip" : "10010" });
> db.addresses.findOne();

{
    "_id" : ObjectId("4e79eeee4a1817c38f000000"),
    "first_name" : "Peter",
    "last_name" : "Parker",
    "address" : "175 Fifth Ave",
    "city" : "New York",
    "state" : "NY",
    "zip" : "10010"
}
```

When using the shell, you can just call ObjectId(), which will return an ObjectId object.

Shell Is JavaScript

The shell doesn't just have a JavaScript interface; it's a full-fledged JavaScript interpreter. You can set variables, write functions, objects, and so on. Often a JavaScript file loaded by the shell is a good way to perform administrative operations, such as loading fixtures, converting data, and others.

Administrative Commands

Although it's beyond the scope of this text, you can run all sorts of administrative commands through the MongoDB shell. Some examples include checking stats, configuring a collection for sharding or shutting down the server.

As an example, here is how one would shut down a server:

```
db._adminCommand("shutdown")
```

Working with Sets

One of the advantages of working with MongoDB is that it retains most of the set functionality of SQL databases. MongoDB has powerful set functionality that easily allows for things like querying ranges, sorting data, paginating data, and more.

Querying Sets

Now that we've established a solid foundation of CRUD (which all operate on a single record), we will introduce working with sets of records. In our previous examples, when we queried we used the method findone, which retrieves one or zero documents. In the following examples, we will use the method find, which retrieves any number of documents. We will also introduce a few more of the operators that will permit querying on ranges.

So far, as we only have a single document in our database, we will use the shell to quickly create 250,000 documents. Just create a PHP file with the following code and run it:

```php
<?php
$conn = new Mongo();
$db = $conn->selectDB('test');
$db->numbers->drop();

for ($i = 0; $i < 250000; $i++) {
    $db->numbers->save(array('num' => $i));
}
?>
```

You could also do this in the shell with the following:

```
use test;
db.numbers.drop();
for(i=0; i < 250000; i++) {
    db.numbers.save({num: i});
}
```

Finding (Querying) Data in MongoDB

As stated earlier, MongoDB is both flexible and easy to work with. Now that we have a set of data, let's ask for the first two records. We will write a query with a limit that will return a MongoCursor Object. We will need to iterate over this object to access the data on contains:

```php
$results = $db->numbers->find()->limit(2);

foreach ($results as $document){
    print_r($document);
}
```

And the output is:

```
Array
(
    [_id] => MongoId Object
        (
            [$id] => 4e7b32174a18176795000000
        )
    [num] => 0
)
Array
(
    [_id] => MongoId Object
        (
            [$id] => 4e7b32174a18176795000001
        )
    [num] => 1
)
```

We are just barely scratching the surface of what the MongoCursor can do.

Pagination with the Cursor

The MongoDB cursor makes pagination easy. These cursor methods can be chained off of the cursor object that find returns and each other. Combining limit with skip makes pagination easy. These can also be combined with order. Extending the example from the previous section:

```
$db->numbers->find()->limit(2)->skip(20)->sort(array('num'=> -1));

foreach ($results as $document){
    print_r($document);
}
```

results in the output:

```
Array
(
    [_id] => MongoId Object
        (
            [$id] => 4ea78e034a1817dd9103d07b
        )

    [num] => 249979
)
Array
(
    [_id] => MongoId Object
        (
            [$id] => 4ea78e034a1817dd9103d07a
        )

    [num] => 249978
)
```

 Notice that the order of the methods doesn't matter, as the actual query itself isn't performed until it is iterated over.

Ranges

MongoDB has a set of operators to handle range operations. These include $gt, $lt, $gte, and $lte, which stand for greater than, less than, greater than or equal, and less than or equal.

Let's say you want all numbers under 15. Replacing the find in the script from earlier:

```
$results = $db->numbers->find( array( 'num' => array( '$lt' => 15 )));
```

Notice that we used single quotes around $lt so that it is treated as a string rather than a variable. This returns the following expected results:

```
Array
(
    [_id] => MongoId Object
        (
            [$id] => 4e7b32174a18176795000000
        )
    [num] => 0
)

...

Array
(
    [_id] => MongoId Object
        (
            [$id] => 4e7b32174a1817679500000e
        )
    [num] => 14
)
```

Working with Arrays

Just like ranges, MongoDB comes with a set of operators for working with arrays; these include $all, $in, $nin, and $size.

Finding a Value in an Array

To find any record that has a value in an array, simply query for it:

```
$set = $addresses->find(
        array( 'superpowers' => 'agility')
    );
```

The power of a flexible schema is revealed here. This query will match any document that has a key superpowers set to the value agility or to an array that contains the value *agility*. You are welcome to mix and match. A good example of when this mixing of types may be useful is if you were writing a CMS system in which most articles have a single author but occasionally people co-author an article. In this example, the query would return the expected results regardless.

$in

The introduction of arrays as a data type opens a realm of new possibilities. Just like in SQL, you can provide a set of values to return multiple documents (records). $in is analgous to SQL's IN in this manner. However, unlike SQL, it can also be used to query against an array. When querying against an array, the document matches when any of the values match any of the values in $in.

The first example should feel very familiar, as its usage is similar to SQL. It would read "find me any record who has a state with the value NY or CA." The fact that our data set doesn't include any values of CA is irrelevant, and it results in the expected response of all records with NY as a state.

```
$set = $addresses->find(
        array( 'state' =>
            array('$in' =>
                array('NY', 'CA')
            )
        )
    );
```

The following example will return all the current entries in our address collection, as all entries have either the value flight or agility in their superpowers array:

```
$set = $addresses->find(
        array( 'superpowers' =>
            array('$in' =>
                array('flight', 'agility')
            )
        )
    );
```

$nin

$nin stands for Not In. It's the opposite of $in and can be used in both ways mentioned earlier. Be aware, though, that if not used carefully it can return a large number of documents or expensive queries, so please use with care.

This example returns only the Clark Kent record, as we have excluded the other records, which have either agility or web crawling in their values.

```
$set = $addresses->find(
        array( 'superpowers' =>
            array('$nin' =>
                array('agility', 'wall crawling' )
            )
        )
    );
```

$all

$all works similar to $in. It permits you to query against an array, but unlike $in, it will return only documents whose array contains all of the values provided. The array in the document may contain more values than those provided but must have the provided values to match. In short, $in uses *or* where $all uses *and*. It's important to know that unlike $in or $nin, $all—because it requires all values—won't match a single value (unless there is only one value in your $all array, in which case you shouldn't use it anyway).

If we took the earlier $in example and changed it to $all, it would result in a null set, as none of the records have both flight and agility. Instead, we will use a pretty specific criteria that will result in the Peter Parker record:

```
$set = $addresses->find(
        array( 'superpowers' =>
            array('$all' =>
                array('agility', 'spidey sense')
            )
        )
    );
```

Matching Entire Arrays

If you want an array to match all and only the values provided, then no operator is
needed—simply query on an array with an array. This is similar to the first example
used, but rather than setting the key to a single value, we will pass in an array. This
requires it to be a perfect and complete match instead of searching for any value in the
array. Because it is looking for an exact match and not comparing value by value, the
order is important. It must be in the same order for it to match.

```
$set = $addresses->find(
        array( 'superpowers' =>
            array (
                    'agility',
                    'stamina',
                    'spidey sense',
                    'web shooters',
                    'superhuman strength',
                    'superhuman intelligence',
                    'wall crawling',
                    'really really good looking',
            )
        )
    );
```

$slice

$slice gives one the ability to retrieve only a section of an array. It is useful in situations
such as when a blog post document has an embedded array of comments but you want
to show only 20 on a page. $slice can either take a single value or an array. The single
value returns that number of elements, in which the array takes two parameters, of
which the first parameter is skip and the second is how many to return. Operating on
our address example from earlier, here is the syntax for both approaches. It's important
to note that this will return the entire document (every key), but in the key, the
$slice operator is used on it will return only the slice specified.

```
$addresses->find(array(),array('superpowers' => array('$slice' => 2)));
$addresses->find(array(),array('superpowers' => array('$slice' => array(2, 3))));
```

The output of the first line (only one document) is:

```
Array (
    [_id] => MongoId Object (
            [$id] => 4ea8b8344a181784a1000001
        )
    [first_name]    => Eliot
```

```
        [last_name]    => Horowitz
        [address]      => 134 Fifth Ave
        [city]         => New York
        [state]        => NY
        [zip]          => 10010
        [superpowers] => Array (
                [0] => agility
                [1] => super human intelligence
            )
    )
)
```

If you want to retrieve only the slice itself and not the entire document, you can come pretty close by retrieving the _id and the slice:

```
print_r($addresses->findone(
    array( 'first_name' => 'Peter', 'last_name' => 'Parker'),
    array('_id' => 1, 'superpowers' => array('$slice' => 2))));
```

which results in:

```
Array (
    [_id] => MongoId Object (
            [$id]   => 4ea8b8344a181784a1000001
        )
    [superpowers] => Array (
            [0] => agility
            [1] => super human intelligence
        )
)
```

$size

$size is a very specific operator with limited use. It will query for the exact number of elements in an array. It doesn't use an index (though the query can still use an index on other criteria) and cannot be used in ranges.

This example will return any document that has five elements in the superpowers array, which in our data set would result in the Clark Kent document.

```
$set = $addresses->find(
        array( 'superpowers' =>
            array('$size' => 5)
        )
    );
```

$elemMatch

Say you wanted to match a city and state in a address array nested within a person's document. While it's not likely, it is possible that they may have a home in Westport, Connecticut, and work in New York, New York. If you simply searched for address.city = "Westport" and address.state = "CT", you would find not only this document but any document in which a city "Westport" existed in any address and any document in which state "CT" existed. Even if you use $and, you would get any document that has both present in any of the elements, but not necessarily the same element. $elemMatch lets you specify that you want all of the provided conditions to exist in the same element of an array.

So far, we haven't created any documents that have nested nested arrays. Here's a document and the $elemMatch query to match.

Note that it will match only documents where there is a locations array and inside of one (or more) of the entries in that array, the key's state and city both exist and are set to "NY" and "New York", respectively.

```
$tengen = array(
    'name' => '10gen',
    'locations' => array(
        array(
            'street no' => '100',
            'street'    => 'Marine Parkway',
            'suite'     => '175',
            'city'      => 'Redwood City',
            'state'     => 'CA',
            'zip'       => '94065'
        ),
        array(
            'street no' => '134',
            'street'    => '5th Avenue',
            'floor'     => '3rd',
            'city'      => 'New York',
            'state'     => 'NY',
            'zip'       => '10011'
        ),
));

$db->company->save($tengen);

$set = $db->company->find( array('locations' => array( '$elemMatch' => array( 'state'
=> 'NY', 'city' => 'New York') )));
```

Using Dot Notation

If you want to select a specific key nested inside of an array, the easiest approach is to use dot notation. While PHP doesn't support dot notation, MongoDB does.

It's important to remember that this is the established way to query keys inside of an (associated) array. Remember that we can't just pass in an array, because that would do an exact comparison. We can't just pass in the value, because it's nested inside an array.

Using the $tengen example from earlier, we could query that structure with dot notation:

```
$db->company->find( array('locations.zip' => '10011'));
```

Conditionals

MongoDB provides a full set of operators for boolean logic. These include $or, $nor, $not, $and, and $exists and can be nested and combined with other operators to create any combination. The $and operator was introduced in 2.0.

It's important to note that these operators should only be used when working with different keys. If working with the same keys, $in and $nin are more efficient.

The following example can be read as "Find me all records that have either the state *NY* or the city *New York* and either the first name *Eliot* or the last name *Parker*."

In our data set, it would result in both documents with *NY* as a state:

```
$set = $addresses->find(
    array( '$and' => array(
        array('$or' => array(
            array('state' => 'NY'),
            array('city' => 'New York')
            )
        ),
        array('$or' => array(
            array('first_name' => 'Eliot'),
            array('last_name' => 'Parker')
            )
        )
    ))
);
```

Working with Multiple Documents

MongoDB permits you to run updates and deletions on multiple documents at the same time.

Updating Multiple Records

By default the update (or save) methods only work on a single document. Both have an additional parameter that accepts an array of options. To update all documents that match the criteria provided, simply pass in array("multiple" => true) in the third parameter.

> Multiple updates are individually atomic, but not atomic as a group. MongoDB doesn't have the ability to have atomicity across the update set, but each individual document will be updated atomically.
>
> A Multiple update is also nonblocking, meaning that other updates can happen while the update is occurring, even on the same data. The way to prevent this is to provide the $atomic option, which confusingly isn't atomic, but isolated. When set to true, the multi update (or delete) will be blocking, ensuring that no other operations happen during this operation on that data set.

Deleting Multiple Records

remove provides the same "options" parameter; however, by default, remove operates on multiple records, so no additional action is needed. If you want to limit it to one document, the justOne option set to true will do the trick.

Working with Indexes

MongoDB uses indexes in much the same way as MySQL and PostgreSQL do. For the most part, all the knowledge you've obtained from working with relational databases will apply to MongoDB. Like most relational databases, MongoDB utilizes a BTree index. There are a few unique features of a document database that have special behaviors. Specifically, due to the flexible schema, not all documents have the same fields. Additionally, documents can contain nested arrays that themselves contain keys and values. Indexes can be applied not only to values, but also to arrays.

Another ported feature from SQL is explain. It works in a similar manner, but takes a more standard object-oriented approach. Simply write the find (or findone) statement as usual and append the explain function call to it:

```
print_r( $db->numbers->find(
            array('num' => array( '$gt' => 50000, '$lt' => 50002))
        )->explain()
);
```

It would give us the following result:

```
Array
(
    [cursor] => BasicCursor
    [nscanned] => 250000
    [nscannedObjects] => 250000
    [n] => 1
    [millis] => 159
    [nYields] => 0
    [nChunkSkips] => 0
    [isMultiKey] =>
    [indexOnly] =>
    [indexBounds] => Array()
    [allPlans] => Array
        (
            [0] => Array
                (
                    [cursor] => BasicCursor
                    [indexBounds] => Array()
                )
        )
    [oldPlan] => Array
        (
            [cursor] => BasicCursor
            [indexBounds] => Array()
```

```
        )
    )
```

Please take note of a couple things. It had to scan the entire collection to return the single document, which took 159 milliseconds. It didn't use an index as evidenced by the "BasicCursor" being used.

How can we make this very inefficient query run better? The answer is obvious: add an index.

Setting Indexes

In MongoDB, setting indexes is easy to do. A single statement will do the trick. Note that with large data sets, it will take a while to create an index.

```
$db->numbers->ensureindex(array( 'num' => 1 ));
```

Placing that above our explain from earlier and running it again will produce a noticeable difference:

```
Array
(
    [cursor] => BtreeCursor num_1
    [nscanned] => 1
    [nscannedObjects] => 1
    [n] => 1
    [millis] => 2
    [nYields] => 0
    [nChunkSkips] => 0
    [isMultiKey] =>
    [indexOnly] =>
    [indexBounds] => Array
        (
            [num] => Array
                (
                    [0] => Array
                        (
                            [0] => 50000
                            [1] => 50002
                        )
                )
        )

    [allPlans] => Array
        (
            [0] => Array
                (
                    [cursor] => BtreeCursor num_1
                    [indexBounds] => Array
                        (
                            [num] => Array
                                (
                                    [0] => Array
                                        (
```

```
                                                [0] => 50000
                                                [1] => 50002
                                          )
                                    )
                              )
                        )
                  )
            )
```

Now the `find` statement has a "BtreeCursor" cursor type and is able to run in 1 millisecond. Thanks to the index, it scanned exactly one object.

Index Order

Indexes can be created in either ascending or descending order. 1 is the default and is ascending; –1 is descending. Using descending order is useful in a few cases. One in particular is dates when typically accessing the most recent data.

About Indexes

A proper understanding of indexes is one of the most important things for a developer to have, and it is so often overlooked. The proper use of indexes is critical to any well-functioning application. Using indexes will enable more efficient use of memory and minimize the amount of time the database spends on disk. MongoDB represents indexes internally as a BTree, which is common in many relational databases. In fact, for most things dealing with indexes in MongoDB, traditional relational logic fully applies. Just like traditional databases, indexes can speed up queries, but will slow down writes. MongoDB only uses one index per query and tries to pick the most optimal one. Every collection automatically contains one index on the `_id` field. Indexes can also be used to maintain uniqueness, as does the one on `_id`.

Compound Indexes

MongoDB supports compound indexes. If you commonly query on two fields—say, state and city—then you should create a compound index containing both fields. You wouldn't want to create two indexes (one on each), as only one would be used and either one would result in a fair amount of scanning on disk. In creating and using compound indexes, order matters. In this example, you would want to make sure that you create the index with state to the left. The syntax for creating a compound index is by simply passing an array to the ensure index method. The following example would be useful when searching for blog posts in a given time range where a specific author commented:

```
$blogpost->ensureIndex(array(
    "ts" => -1,

    "comments.author" => 1
```

```
    ));
```

Indexing Arrays

Again, in MongoDB, the addition of an array as a data type provides interesting possibilities. MongoDB permits indexing of arrays in two different ways:

1. You could index the entire array. In this case, it will treat it as a whole and compare against the entire array top to bottom and left to right.
2. You could index the keys and values of an array. In this case, it will treat them individually.

Indexes and Memory

As stated earlier, MongoDB was designed for modern systems and applications. As many systems today are multicore machines with copious amounts of memory, MongoDB is written to takes full advantage of them. MongoDB works most efficiently when indexes and working data fit into memory. If as your data set grows you begin to notice performance degradation, more than likely it is the result of your memory being too small to contain your working data set or indexes. At a minimum, you should ensure that your indexes fit into memory.

There is one exception to this, and it's pretty specific but not altogether uncommon—if your data is sequentially inserted and sequentially read. A logging application in which the working data is only the most recent segment of data is a good example. This application can get away with having only the working data set and the portion of the index needed to support that working data set in memory.

It's important to realize that MongoDB will use as much memory as you can give it. One way to think of MongoDB is that it is both a persistent database as well as a memory cache (like Memcache). It will benefit greatly from more memory as it is accomplishing both of these functions.

Database References

While MongoDB is not a relational database, it does support a kind of relationship called references.

MongoDB does have a defined reference called a DBRef, which is simply an array with two specific elements. Unlike ObjectId and MongoDate, it is not a new type, but rather a defined convention that the drivers understand. The two required elements are $ref ⇒ "collection name" and $id the primary key (ObjectId) in that collection and the order matters and must be in the order specified here.

As it is only a convention, application developers are welcome to use their own conventions if it better suits their purposes (and it often does). Often the need to store the collection is unnecessary as they are typically consistent across similar documents. In these cases, it would be better to store it in the application somewhere like a model object.

DBRefs can optionally store more data as needed (it's just an array, after all). Sometimes it's helpful to reference a document but store a slug/snippet/thumbnail on the reference itself as easy access without accessing the entire other document.

References Are Not Foreign Keys

In a relational database (at least an unsharded one), foreign keys serve many purposes, one of which is ensuring that the data contained has integrity. Databases ensure that foreign keys don't reference data that isn't present; in other words, ensure you don't delete data that has references to it. A reference is simply a pointer and shares none of those properties. In fact, you can create a reference to a document that doesn't even exist.

Additionally, foreign keys with join statements enable you to patch together different parts of data as if it were all one table on which you can sort and perform different operations. In MongoDB, a reference is simply a pointer and doesn't provide this feature either.

When to Use References or Reference versus Embed

As a warning, this topic isn't very complex, but isn't altogether intuitive and is very specific to the application. There is no "one size fits all" or even "one size fits many" here. I'll provide some guidelines, but proper application would depend largely on data set, data usage, access patterns, and data size.

Now that we've fully covered what references are and aren't, you're probably wondering when you would use a reference. Often you'll be asking if a given piece of data should be a reference or an embedded document. The following guidelines can hopefully provide insight into the best implementation for your application. Figure 2-1 shows when to use a reference instead of an embedded document.

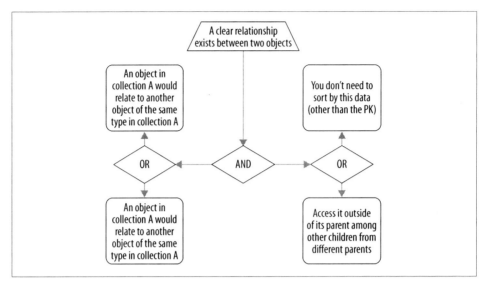

Figure 2-1. When to use a reference versus embedding

Typically, the approach is to use an embedded array unless there is a clear reason for doing otherwise.

How to Create References

There are two different approaches to references. You can use manual references or DBRefs. Manual references are primary keys, whereas a DBRef is a pointer to specific document and collection. The general rule is that if your referenced collection will always be the same, the manual references are more convenient.

Creating Manual References

Creating manual references is as simple as storing a primary key of another document and using findOne to access it:

```
$post = array(
    'title' => 'MongoDB and PHP',
    'text' => 'MongoDB an PHP are like PB and J. Good alone, great together',
    'author' => 'spf13'
);

$post2 = array(
    '_id' => $id,
    'title' => 'MongoDB, PHP and You',
    'text' => 'Before MongoDB I felt so empty using PHP. Now I have a new lease on life',
    'author' => 'spf13'
);

$user = array(
```

```
    '_id'  => 'spf13',
    'name' => 'Steve Francia'
);


$db->articles->insert($post, true);
$db->articles->insert($post2);
$db->users->insert($user);

foreach ( $db->articles->find(array('author' => $user['_id'])) as $p) {
    print_r($p);
}
```

Creating DBRefs

MongoDB provides a `createDBRef` method that accepts two parameters. The first is the name of the collection and the second is either the ID or the object of the referenced document. The following example will create two documents, each referencing each other. Notice how in the example we actually create the reference to the second document before it is even created. This saves us from a third operation of having to update the first document.

```
$id = new MongoId();

$post = array(
    'title'   => 'MongoDB and PHP',
    'text'    => 'MongoDB an PHP are like PB and J. Good alone, great together.',
    'related' => array($db->createDBRef('articles', $id))
    );

$post2 = array(
    '_id'     => $id,
    'title'   => 'MongoDB, PHP and You',
    'text'    => 'Before MongoDB I felt so empty using PHP. Now I have a new lease on
life',
    'related' => array($db->createDBRef('articles', $post))
    );

$db->articles->insert($post);
$db->articles->insert($post2);

foreach( $db->articles->find() as $p) {
    print_r($p);
}
```

Either of the two previous examples would return the same two documents. This output is from the second one to illustrate the structure of the DBRef:

```
Array
(
    [_id] => MongoId Object
        (
            [$id] => 4e80f9ef4a181706c7000001
        )
```

```
        [title] => MongoDB and PHP
        [text] => MongoDB an PHP are like PB and J. Good alone, great together.
        [author] => spf13
        [related] => Array
            (
                [0] => Array
                    (
                        [$ref] => articles
                        [$id] => MongoId Object
                            (
                                [$id] => 4e80f9ef4a181706c7000000
                            )
                    )
            )
    )
Array
(
    [_id] => MongoId Object
        (
            [$id] => 4e80f9ef4a181706c7000000
        )

    [title] => MongoDB, PHP and You
    [text] => Before MongoDB I felt so empty using PHP. Now I have a new lease on life
    [author] => spf13
    [related] => Array
        (
            [0] => Array
                (
                    [$ref] => articles
                    [$id] => MongoId Object
                        (
                            [$id] => 4e80f9ef4a181706c7000001
                        )
                )
        )
)
```

How to Access DBRefs

The getDBRef method takes a DBRef array and returns the referenced document:

```
print_r($db->getDBRef($post2['related'][0]));
```

This results in the expected document ($post from earlier):

```
Array
(
    [_id] => MongoId Object
        (
            [$id] => 4e81d1f94a1817ed05000001
        )

    [title] => MongoDB and PHP
```

```
[text] => MongoDB an PHP are like PB and J. Good alone, great together
[related] => Array
    (
        [0] => Array
            (
                [$ref] => articles
                [$id] => MongoId Object
                    (
                        [$id] => 4e81d1f94a1817ed05000000
                    )
            )
    )
)
```

Dates and Times

It's important to make a note of how MongoDB handles dates. As PHP and many other languages (including JavaScript) don't have a native date type, MongoDB uses a date object called MongoDate. If no value is passed in, it will use the current date and time.

```
// save a date to the database
$collection->save(array("created" => new MongoDate()));
```

You can also specify dates by passing in a Unix timestamp, like that generated by strtotime:

```
$birth = new MongoDate(strtotime("1953-04-13 00:00:00"));
```

MongoDate can be passed into the date method for easy use in your application:

```
date('Y-M-d h:m:s', $mongodate->sec);
```

 MongoDate stores dates as the number of milliseconds since the epoch (similar to Unix time, which stores seconds since the epoch). This means that it has millisecond accuracy and — like Unix time — ignores time zones.

CHAPTER 3

Advanced MongoDB

Now that you have the basics down, you should feel quite ready to build most applications, or at least the majority of functionality in any application. This section will take you into deeper functionality, enabling you to do even more with MongoDB. We will cover regular expressions, aggregation, MapReduce, replication, and sharding.

Regular Expressions

In addition to all of the logical operators provided, MongoDB also provides a full regular expression (regex) engine. Regular expressions are run against strings and between the two, there really isn't any query you can't create (within a single collection; across multiple collections, you've got MapReduce and client logic at your disposal).

To best illustrate the usage of regular expressions and how they pertain to indexes, we will use a data set of colors:

```
$db->colors->save(array('color' => 'red'));
$db->colors->save(array('color' => 'blue'));
$db->colors->save(array('color' => 'green'));
$db->colors->save(array('color' => 'purple'));
$db->colors->save(array('color' => 'orange'));
$db->colors->save(array('color' => 'turquoise'));
$db->colors->save(array('color' => 'black'));
$db->colors->save(array('color' => 'brown'));
$db->colors->save(array('color' => 'teal'));
$db->colors->save(array('color' => 'silver'));
$db->colors->save(array('color' => 'tan'));
$db->colors->save(array('color' => 'navy'));
$db->colors->save(array('color' => 'yellow'));
$db->colors->save(array('color' => 'indigo'));

$db->colors->ensureIndex('color');
```

Creating a MongoDB Regular Expression

MongoDB uses Perl Compatible Regular Expressions (PCRE) regular expressions, the same ones used in PHP and JavaScript. MongoDB currently supports six flags:

i

> Case insensitive

m

> Multiline

x

> Can contain comments

l

> Locale

s

> Dotall (".") matches everything, including newlines

u

> Match unicode

MongoDB provides the MongoRegex object to create MongoDB regular expressions:

```
$db->colors->find(array( 'color' => new MongoRegex('/^b/')));
```

Regular Expressions and Indexes

Regular expressions can take full advantage of indexes if present. It's important to understand how indexes work to take advantage of them. BTree's compare left to right. This means that your regular expression will take advantages of indexes when it is comparing the beginning of the string. If you use wildcards at the beginning, and literals in the middle or end, it will have to do a full table scan, as the index is of no help. The previous example takes full advantages of indexes. Running `explain` will help you see if your query is performing as intended:

```
print_r( $db->colors->find(
        array( 'color' => new MongoRegex('/^b/')))->explain()
    );
```

This code results in the following output:

```
Array (
    [cursor] => BtreeCursor color_1 multi
    [nscanned] => 4
    [nscannedObjects] => 3
    [n] => 3
    [millis] => 0
    ...
```

The important things to look for are the "nscanned" and "n." You will notice that in this output, they are very close. Ideally, you would want them to be as close as possible.

If we didn't use the index, you would see "[cursor] ⇒ BasicCursor" instead.Now what if we look for the last letter, any color ending with "e"?

```
print_r( $db->colors->find(
        array( 'color' => new MongoRegex('/e$/')))->explain()
    );
```

You will notice that it is still using an index, but it can't find the best path and is now doing a full index scan. While a full index scan is better than a full table scan, it doesn't provide nearly the performance proper index utilization does.

```
Array (
    [cursor] => BtreeCursor color_1 multi
    [nscanned] => 14
    [nscannedObjects] => 4
    [n] => 4
    [millis] => 0
    ...
```

The first example is really the only way to fully utilize an index. Additionally, it must be done without the "i" switch, as the index isn't case-insensitive and will need to do a full table scan.

Aggregation Commands

Certain functionality is extended to MongoDB through the use of commands. These work well as the drivers become forward-compatible as new features are added. Currently, the functionality includes aggregation functionality such as group, dis tinct, and MapReduce; it also provides operational functionality like "get last error" as well as administrative functions like "shutdown" or "get profiling level." This section will focus on the aggregation functionality provided by MongoDB.

The Distinct Command

Distinct reproduces the corresponding functionality in SQL. It has many uses, none of which are unique to MongoDB. A good example use would be to provide a list of all tags used on blog posts. The following example will show all superpowers in the address book using the data we created in the previous chapter. The Distinct command returns more than just the anticipated values as shown here. Be sure to access the values array and not the entire returned array.

```
print_r($db->command(
    array("distinct" => "addresses",
    "key" => "superpowers")
));

Array
(
    [values] => Array
        (
```

```
            [0] => agility
            [1] => spidey sense
            [2] => stamina
            [3] => super human intelligence
            [4] => super human strength
            [5] => wall crawling
            [6] => web shooters
        )

    [stats] => Array
        (
            [n] => 2
            [nscanned] => 2
            [nscannedObjects] => 2
            [timems] => 0
        )

    [ok] => 1
)
```

Distinct will take full advantage of an index if one exists; in fact, if it is able to, it will retrieve all values from the index and never actually touch the collection.

Distinct is limited to returning a single BSON object's worth of data, which is equal to the maximum document size: either 16 MB or 4 MB, depending on the MongoDB version.

The Group Command

The MongoDB cursor also provides the ability to group data similar to the "GROUP BY" functionality of SQL. The group command can best be viewed as a simpler version of MapReduce (covered later in this chapter).

group comes with three fairly serious limitations:

1. It operates only on data sizes of 10,000 unique keys or less.
2. It is limited to returning a single document worth of data (4 MB in 1.6 and lower, 16 MB in 1.8 and higher).
3. It doesn't work in sharded environments.

MapReduce does not suffer from any of these limitations and should be used as a substitute whenever anticipating any of these situations.

One would wonder why to use group at all. As long as the three limitations are not a hindrance, then it operates a measurable amount faster than MapReduce while also providing a slightly simpler interface to work with.

Group Parameters

The group command takes three required parameters:

key
> The fields to group by in an array or object. Also accepts a function (MongoCode). You would use a function if you wanted to group by day of the week, for example.

initial
> The initial value of the aggregation counter object. This is usually a value set to 0 or to an empty array.

reduce
> The reduce function is a JavaScript function that aggregates the iterated objects. Typical operations of a reduce function include summing and counting. It performs a similar role as the reduce function in MapReduce but operates differently. This reduce function always takes two arguments, the current iterated document and the aggregation counter object.

The fourth parameter can be:

condition
> A find() query that needs to be true for the current iterating document to be considered in the aggregation.

finalize
> An optional function to be run on each item in the result set just before the item is returned. Can either modify the item (e.g., add an average field given a count and a total) or return a replacement object (returning a new object with just _id and average fields).

Group Examples

Let's create a simple data set to group against:

```
$connection = new Mongo();
$db = $connection->selectDB('dbname');

$db->animals->drop();
$db->animals->save(array("class" => 'mammal', 'name' => 'kangaroo'));
$db->animals->save(array("class" => 'mammal', 'name' => 'seal'));
$db->animals->save(array("class" => 'mammal', 'name' => 'dog'));
$db->animals->save(array("class" => 'bird', 'name' => 'eagle'));
$db->animals->save(array("class" => 'bird', 'name' => 'ostrich'));
$db->animals->save(array("class" => 'bird', 'name' => 'emu'));
$db->animals->save(array("class" => 'reptile', 'name' => 'snake'));
$db->animals->save(array("class" => 'reptile', 'name' => 'turtle'));
$db->animals->save(array("class" => 'amphibian', 'name' => 'frog'));
```

First, here's a simple example. This example is simply grouping each animal into a class:

```
$reduce = new MongoCode(<<<'EOF'
function(doc,counter) {
    counter.items.push(obj.name);
}
EOF
);
```

```
$g = $db->animals->group(
    array('class' => 1),
    array('items' => array()),
    $reduce
);

echo json_encode($g['retval']);
```

and results in the following output. Notice that for brevity's sake, I've converted the output to JSON.

```
[{"class":"mammal","items":["kangaroo","seal","dog"]},
 {"class":"bird","items":["eagle","ostrich","emu"]},
 {"class":"reptile","items":["snake","turtle"]},
 {"class":"amphibian","items":["frog"]}]
```

Now say you wanted to count the number of animals in each class. This code:

```
$reduce = new MongoCode('function(doc,counter) {
    counter.count++;
}');

$g = $db->animals->group(
    array('class' => 1),
    array('count' => 0),
    $reduce
);
echo json_encode($g['retval']);
```

results in the following output:

```
[{"class":"mammal","count":3},
 {"class":"bird","count":3},
 {"class":"reptile","count":2},
 {"class":"amphibian","count":1}]
```

MapReduce

MapReduce is a fairly popular approach used to distribute computing across many threads or nodes (see Figure 3-1). MongoDB supports MapReduce. There are some common misconceptions about MapReduce, one of which is that it is an approach to do operations faster. This isn't accurate. MapReduce is designed to handle extremely large data sets and does a great job at doing so. It doesn't, however, guarantee speed.

Overview

MapReduce is a framework for processing problems across large data sets using many nodes for massive parallelization. Inspired by functional programming, it was introduced by Google in 2004. It primarily consists of a map function to be run many times in parallel and a reduce function that takes the output (emits) from all the maps and "reduces" them down to a single value for each key or in the case of emitting an array, a set of values for each key. Each implementation of MapReduce is slightly different,

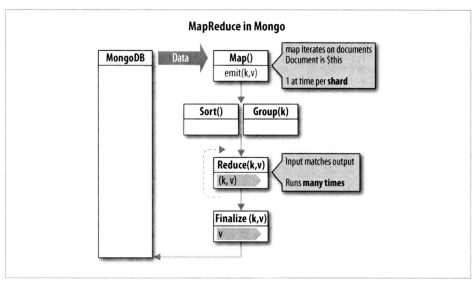

Figure 3-1. MapReduce in MongoDB

and MongoDB is no exception. In MongoDB, only two methods are required: the Map and Reduce methods. Additional helper methods are also available to group, sort, and finalize the data. It's important to recognize that all of these methods are JavaScript, regardless of the client language, and are executed on the database server.

The syntax for MapReduce looks like this:

```
$ck = array(
    'first_name' => 'Clark',
    'last_name'  => 'Kent',
    'address'    => '344 Clinton St., Apt. #3B',
    'city'       => 'Metropolis',
    'state'      => 'IL',
    'zip'        => '62960',
    'superpowers' => array( 'superhuman strength', 'invulnerability', 'flight',
'superhuman speed', 'heat vision' )
    );

$addresses->save($ck);❶

$map = new MongoCode("function() { emit(this.state,1); }");❷
$reduce = new MongoCode(<<<'EOD'❸
function(k, vals) {
    var sum = 0;
    for (var i in vals) {
        sum += vals[i];
    }
    return sum;❹
}
EOD
);
```

```
$mr = $db->command(array(
    "mapreduce" => "addresses",
    "map" => $map,
    "reduce" => $reduce,
    "out" => array("merge" => "stateCounts")));❺

$states = $db->selectCollection($mr['result'])->find();❻
foreach ($states as $state) {
    echo $state['value']." heros live in ". $state['_id'] . "\n";
}
```

❶ Adding another document to the address book we created in Chapter 2.

❷ Defining the map function. It's important to recognize that the MapReduce functions are written in JavaScript and run on the server. The map function references the variable this to inspect the current document. Inside a map function, emit(key,value) is called once for every value wanting to be fed to the reducer. In most cases, this will only be one time (as the example here), but if we wanted to count superpowers (or for a blog, tags), we would call it multiple times (or even no times if no superpowers existed).

❸ Defining the reduce function. Like the map function, it's written in JavaScript. The reduce function takes an array of all the emitted values and reduces them into a single value. This is commonly used to aggregate data to produce things like sums. Please note we are using a nowdoc here to enclose the function in a string.

❹ In this simple example, it's easy to miss that the value returned by the reduce function matches the structure as the document emitted by the map function. In the example, it's a single value, but if map emitted an array (the second parameter in the emit function call), then reduce would need to return an array. This is because the reduce function may be run multiple times over the same document until it is done reducing.

❺ It has four possible values: "inline" => 1, "replace" => collectionName, "reduce" => collectionName, and "merge" => collection Name. Inline causes the command to return the data itself instead of a cursor object. replace replaces the output collection entirely (drop and create). merge keeps existing values and replaces them with new values when the keys match. reduce keeps existing values and uses the reduce function to reduce them to a single value when keys match.

❻ Because we used one of the methods that creates a collection, we need to perform a find on the collection, then iterate over the cursor find returns.

The biggest limitation of MongoDB's MapReduce implementation is that it runs on the SpiderMonkey JavaScript interpreter, which unfortunately is single-threaded and interpreted (instead of compiled). What this means to you is that MapReduce operations are slower than a compiled command like Distinct. They are also a bit complicated to write.

MapReduce provides the flexibility to do most anything that isn't a built-in function. MapReduce should only be used when built-in methods are unable to accomplish the desired result as the native functions provide a speed improvement and are much simpler to use.

findAndModify

The `findAndModify` command lets you atomically update and return a document in a single operation. There are a handful of very useful use cases for this sort of operation; for example, any time you need to increment a value and return the document with the new value. It's important to recognize that this kind of operation depends on a fully consistent database, which is exactly what MongoDB is.

```
$result = $this->db->command(array(
    'findAndModify' => 'collectionName',
    'query' => array('fieldname' => 'userid'),
    'update' => array('$inc' => array('value' => 1)),
    'upsert' => 1,
    'new' => 1)
);
```

GridFS

One of the less talked about features of MongoDB is GridFS. Despite its great benefits, it is commonly misunderstood and consequently underutilized.

We have been trained to think of a database as a place to store structured data and a file system as a place to store files, but why? In the last few years, this line has become rather fuzzy as operating systems have put more resources into better file systems and storing more metadata and indexing more and more of it. Particularly fuzzy is network file systems, which in a lot of ways, redefine the term "file system." Network file systems are more like a protocol than a file system, but a protocol dedicated to saving and retrieving files.

Unlike traditional filesystems, which organize and expose bits on a drive, network file systems such as NFS, SMB, FTP, HTTP, and so on are implemented using user space daemons. They sit on top of disk file systems that manage all the dirty details of organizing bits on a drive while they focus on `expose` files over a network protocol. GridFS is this type of network file system.

What Is GridFS?

A network file system built on top of MongoDB, GridFS is different from other network filesystems in a few ways:

- It piggybacks on the MongoDBs protocol rather than creating its own.

- It does organize bits, but inside of a MongoDB database.
- It fully supports replication and sharding (or rather works in replicated and sharded environments).
- It can provide horizontal scale (virtually unlimited in size) and high availability.

At its core, it's really a convention for storing files of any size in a MongoDB collection. All of the language drivers are written to this convention.

It's important to note that there aren't any operating system drivers for GridFS (yet). GridFS is fairly rudimentary as far as file systems go. Its bread and butter is the simple operations of put, get, and delete.

To my knowledge, it is the only open source tool of its kind that easily provides a fully replicated file system with automatic fail over and recovery. The additional benefit of expanding the total space through horizontal scaling makes it a very appealing technology.

Using GridFS

A typical use case for GridFS would be storage and retrieval of an avatar for a user. In a common web application and architecture, you would likely have a few web nodes, all of which would need to be able to store and serve from the same set of files. Historically, you may have used NFS for this task, and more than likely, you've been bitten a time or two for doing so. GridFS is perfectly suited for this task. GridFS automatically separates files into acceptable sized chunks of 256KB and creates documents to store the different chunks and, upon retrieval, combines them.

In the following example, we will store a JPEG file into GridFS. The size doesn't matter, as GridFS takes care of all the details. There is a practical limit of what you would pull out of GridFS using PHP as PHP will load the entire file into memory.

The storeFile method will return the primary key of the newly created file:

```
$connection = new Mongo();
$db = $connection->selectDB('photos');

$grid = $db->getGridFS();

// The file's location in the File System

$path = '/tmp/';
$filename = 'masterword.jpg';

$storedfile = $grid->storeFile(
    $path . $filename,
    array( "metadata" => array( "filename" => $filename)),
    array("filename" => $filename)
    );

echo $storedfile;
```

Mongofiles

MongoDB also ships with mongofiles, a command-line utility for working with GridFS. With mongofiles, you can simply list, put, delete, and get files from GridFS without any programming.

The interface is quite straightforward. Here is how we would store an image:

```
$ mongofiles -d images put mastersword.jpg

connected to: 127.0.0.1
added file: { _id: ObjectId('4ea224f255868dc9e6fd85e1'), filename: "mastersword.jpg",
chunkSize: 262144, uploadDate: new Date(1319249138621), md5:
"957d1ff5b3641c35e295a09e47fba3b5", length: 65115 }
done!
```

This code will insert the *mastersword.jpg* image into the images database. For full usage, simply run mongofiles --help.

Replication

MongoDB uses replication to ensure high availability. It takes a similar approach as MySQL and PostgreSQL, in which there is a single master where writes occur. Data written to the master are then replicated to one or more slave nodes. It's important to point out that replication is never a good way to scale. It can help to scale reads in a limited way, but its true purpose is to provide high availability. For scaling MongoDB, see the next section, "Sharding" on page 51.

High Availability

Replica sets are an improvement on the traditional master/slave setup commonly found in databases. Instead of a master and slave, nodes are set up in a replica set, each with awareness of the other members. The terms used for "master" and "slave" have been replaced by "primary" and "secondary" to distinguish them from the traditional "master" and "slave," though there are far more similarities than differences. Replica sets facilitate automatic fail over and automatic recovery of nodes. A replica set consists of at least three nodes with a maximum of eight.

Why Three Nodes?

Many people wonder why the minimum requirement is not two nodes like master/slave. The reason for this is that the replica set needs to be able to establish a majority to determine a primary. This can be accomplished two ways, either with three or more nodes or by using two nodes and an arbiter. Unlike the other nodes, an arbiter doesn't store any data, but is there to cast a vote when a majority is needed. The reason for more than two nodes is pretty simple.

To illustrate, I will use an example in which you have only two nodes, A and B. A is currently serving as the primary and B as the secondary. Something happens so that B cannot see A and A cannot see B. The nodes themselves don't have any way to distinguish whether the other node is up or whether something has happened to their connection. If both assumed that the other was down, then both would become primary, resulting in both simultaneously writing, thus causing collisions. If both assumed that they were unavailable, then both would become secondary and no writes would be permitted. The only way to resolve this is by adding another party (node or arbiter) that can cast a vote. Once we add a third node C, we can now establish a majority. If A and C can talk to each other, then B must be down or otherwise unavailable and will elect a primary from themselves. B, realizing that it is in the minority, will step down (if primary) and once it becomes part of the majority, it will recover.

Really Easy Configuration

If you have ever tried to set up replication with automatic failover and recovery using existing database solutions, you will be familiar with the many challenges this brings. In contrast, MongoDB is extremely easy to set up using the following commands. This is being done using the MongoDB shell. The first block creates the configuration array. In this example, we are using three instances running on different ports on localhost. This command only needs to be run on one of the machines. They will automatically communicate with each other and configure the other nodes.

```
> config = {
  "_id" : "myReplicaSet",
  "members" : [
    { "_id" : 0, "host" : "localhost:54321" },
    { "_id" : 1, "host" : "localhost:54322" },
    { "_id" : 2, "host" : "localhost:54323", "arbiterOnly" : true}
  ]
}
> rs.initiate(config)
```

Checking the Replica Set Status

Checking the status of the replica set is just as easy; simply connect to any of the nodes and run rs.status():

```
> rs.status()
```

This is only intended as a brief introduction into replication with MongoDB. MongoDB also supports tagging and priorities which can be useful when dealing with high availability across multiple data centers.

Sharding

It is not the intent of this text to provide any more than a very basic introduction into how MongoDB scales horizontally through sharding. Please consult the documentation before attempting to implement a sharded system.

MongoDB provides truly horizontal scaling of data through sharding. Combined with replication from the previous section, MongoDB provides a fully consistent, highly available horizontally scaling database system.

For those not familiar with sharding, it is the practice of partitioning data so that data is split across many nodes. Unlike replication, where each node in a replica set contains the same data, in a sharded cluster, the data is sliced into segments and divided among the shards. For example, in a four-node cluster, each shard would have approximately 25% of the data. While a shard could consist of a single node, in most cases each shard would contain a replica set.

The practice of partitioning data across many servers is not new; this technique has long been employed for scaling systems like MySQL. However, with MySQL and similar systems, the responsibility of partitioning the data was left to the DBA or programmer. The programmer would be responsible not only for tracking what pieces were on which system but also for ensuring even distribution of the data on each node. Finally, when more capacity was needed, the programmer would be responsible for manually splitting the data onto the new machine.

MongoDB automatically splits and distributes the data evenly. It also automatically balances the data as new data is created. It automatically redistributes the data when more nodes are added. As the final icing on the cake, the application is blissfully unaware it is communicating with a sharded cluster as the connection is exactly the same whether connecting to a single server or a sharded cluster. If you aren't sold yet, one final selling point is that you can convert from a single replica set to a sharded cluster easily and without any downtime. I can't stress enough that this should be done well before approaching maximum capacity to avoid downtime.

Figure 3-2 illustrates a basic sharded MongoDB architecture. A shard typically consists of at least three nodes as a replica set. The cluster itself requires one or three config servers, which are the brains of the cluster. They store all the meta and routing data for every chunk of data. The last component is the mongos, which is essentially a routing process. The mongos communicates with the config servers and knows where to find each piece of data. It emulates a mongod server, so the application seamlessly communicates with mongos just like it would mongod. So seamless is this operation that the application for all intents and purposes doesn't need to change when going from a single node (or replica set) to a sharded cluster.

The minimum number of nodes required for a highly available shard (with two shards) is nine: three config servers and three times two replica sets. The mongos is a process that can easily run on the application servers and generally should run on the applica-

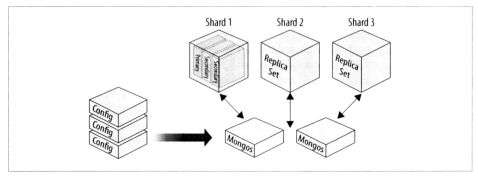

Figure 3-2. A Sharded Architecture

tion servers, as it eliminates a network hop and consumes a modest amount of resources on the machine.

Gotchas

As all languages are different, with different characteristics, each has its own quirks that can sometimes cause friction. PHP has three specific traits that can cause minor issues when working with MongoDB. Specifically, they are: using $ to denote a variable; PHP's unique hybrid array/associative array type; and PHP turning POST variables with names containing "[]" into arrays.

I will cover in detail the potential pitfalls of each and how to avoid them.

The $ Problem

PHP is one of very few languages that use $ to distinguish a variable. MongoDB also makes heavy use of the $ character not for variables, but to distinguish certain keywords used as operators. In general, this isn't much of an issue, provided that the developer is careful to always use single quotes around the operator strings and not double quotes, which would try to evaluate these characters as a variable.

Use:

```
$c->find(array("x" => array('$gt' => 4)));
```

not:

```
$c->find(array("x" => array("$gt" => 4)));
```

This behavior is configurable, but at the expense of consistency with other languages and portability. There is a setting you can put in the *php.ini* file that will change the $ character for MongoDB to whatever you choose. For example, if you wanted to change it to : you would put

```
mongo.cmd = ":"
```

into your *php.ini* file. This setting can also be set using *ini_set()*. The previous line would then become:

```
$c->find(array("x" => array(':gt' => 4)));
```

In my experience, this hasn't been an issue in practice and I've preferred to leave the default character, as it is quite easy to avoid using double quotes.

The Array != Array Problem

PHP also has a property unique among all programming languages. In all other languages, JavaScript included, there is a difference between an key value data construct and an ordered list. In other languages, these go by various names such as "hash" and "dictionary" for the "key" ⇒ "value" and "list" or "array" for the "ordered list." Additionally, in many other languages, order is not guaranteed in the "key" ⇒ "value." In practice, these two systems work quite well in spite of this difference, and in nearly all cases, you would never notice a difference.

Request Injection Attacks

Before you get all worried remembering horror stories about SQL injection attacks, despite the similar name, request injection attacks have little in common, are much less dangerous, and far easier to prevent. In SQL, all operations (select, delete, drop, etc.) are passed to the database as a string into a query method. Additionally, SQL accepts multiple commands in the same request delimited by a semicolon. Because of these two properties, it is very easy to do undesired things in SQL. In MongoDB, each operation has a distinct method which must be explicitly called for that operation. The find method will only find. It won't permit other types of operations. There is also no way to pass in user input that runs additional commands. Because of its explicit nature, the MongoDB interface is far more secure out of the box than SQL.

Due to the dynamic typing of PHP, particularly in how it handles GET and POST variables, it is possible for a parameter to be passed that would permit a user to access undesired data. All a user would need to do is pass in an array instead of a string. For example, instead of username=steve, the user would pass in username[$ne] => 'steve'. PHP will automatically convert this into an array and MongoDB would treat it as one would expect, returning all but the document where username=steve.

It is important to note that this attack can be used in a more malicious manner if used in a remove instead of find.

The good news is that this is quite easy to avoid. Simply cast your GET/POST variables into strings when expecting strings. When removing documents, make sure to use the justOne parameter whenever appropriate.

CHAPTER 4

PHP Libraries and Tools

I hope that by now, you've become excited about how nice the MongoDB driver is to use. We at 10gen have worked extremely hard to make the developer experience as pleasant as possible.

While the MongoDB driver makes it quite easy to use MongoDB from within PHP, you may prefer to add another level of abstraction, particularly with larger applications. One reason for doing so would be to standardize document structure across the application, including data validation.

Many PHP libraries exist to work with MongoDB. I have selected only a handful that I have experience with and that I feel are viable solutions. This list isn't meant to be exhaustive but rather to introduce the reader to libraries that may be able to help them with their projects. I am not endorsing any of these libraries—merely introducing them as potential solutions for the reader.

Object Document Mappers (ODM)

A number of solid Object Document Mappers (ODMs) exist for PHP. The concept is similar to the ORM, but the implementation is significantly different. The ODMs are considerably lighter than any ORM and much much faster. I've listed a few I have experience with here.

Disclaimer: Doctrine development is sponsored by OpenSky, the social ecommerce website, where I worked as the VP of engineering. In spite of this relationship, I've endeavored to be as impartial as possible in my introduction to these libraries.

Doctrine MongoDB ODM

Doctrine was the first viable ORM for PHP. Unlike prior solutions, which followed the active record model, Doctrine took its inspiration from Hibernate for Java. Doctrine2 is an ambitious project that has resulted in a faster and more efficient library.

Concurrent with the development of Doctrine2, the NoSQL movement began to pick up steam, and as an extension of the Doctrine project, Doctrine MongoDB ODM was born.

Doctrine MongoDB ODM leverages the rich set of features Doctrine provides to enable things like validation and events. It allows you to create objects that transparently persist to MongoDB while retaining the same style of objects and behavior as the Doctrine ORM project. In fact, you can even create a single object that has elements persisted in each backend. OpenSky used this feature to use a hybrid of MongoDB and MySQL to add transactional support for our orders. See *http://www.spf13.com/presentations* for details.

Doctrine supports the following features:

- Provides full validation
- Seamless integration with Doctrine ORM
- Useful for hybrid solutions
- Follows same persistence model as Doctrine
- Uses a Document Manager and annotations
- Supports embedded and referenced objects
- Can use mongo's query interface
- Supports in place updates

Doctrine MongoDB ODM can be found at *https://github.com/doctrine/mongodb-odm*.

Active Mongo

Active Mongo seeks to take the MongoDB interface—which returns arrays—even further, utilizing the Active Record paradigm. In addition to providing the friendly interface that comes with Active Record, one of the big features Active Mongo provides is automatically calculating the diff and performing in place updates. Many of the alternatives would set the entire document each time, whereas Active Mongo ensures that the minimal amount is changed.

Active Mongo supports a simple filter mechanism that it uses for validation.

Active Mongo supports the following features:

- Uses Active Record (active document) interface
- Supports full validation

- Supports in place updating
- Uses native query interface
- Supports referenced documents

Active Mongo can be found at *https://github.com/crodas/ActiveMongo*.

Mandango

Mandango was built for speed. Specifically, it was written to be as simple and fast as possible. Given the lean approach, it boasts a fairly significant feature set:

- Very light and fast
- Event support
- Supports embedded and referenced objects
- Uses the mongo query syntax
- Lacking validation, but events can be utilized to validate

Mandango is located at *https://github.com/mandango/mandango*.

Tools

Various tools exist for MongoDB. I've only included ones here that are PHP based, but as they provide support and operate independent of your application, they really could be any language.

MongoQueue

MongoQueue is an (asynchronous) queuing system using nothing but PHP and MongoDB. It's an excellent and popular use case for MongoDB and a great fit for PHP.

MongoQueue supports the following features:

- Fully configurable
- Distributed
- Atomic locking
- Priority support
- Worker timeout support
- Stable

MongoQueue can be found at *https://github.com/skiz/mongo_queue*.

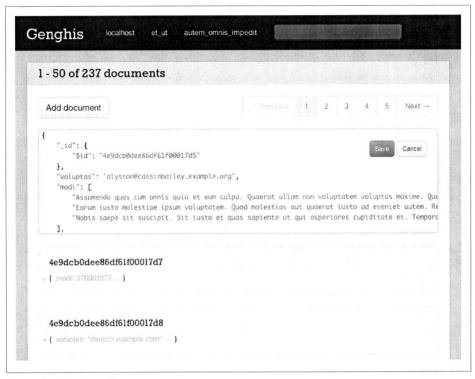

Figure 4-1. Genghis edit screen

Genghis

Genghis is a PHP frontend for MongoDB, similar in nature to PHPMyAdmin (see Figure 4-1). Genghis boasts single-file installation and a very usable interface.

Genghis can be found at *https://genghisapp.com*.

RockMongo

RockMongo is similar to Genghis except that it is more mature and isn't quite as pretty. RockMongo can be found at *http://code.google.com/p/rock-php/wiki/rock_mongo*.

Frameworks

As many projects today are not written from scratch, but rather jump-started by using an existing framework, I'll briefly describe the current state of frameworks as it pertains to MongoDB. As counsel, many factors should go into choosing which framework to use for a project and support for a specific database, while it may be a factor, shouldn't be the only factor.

Even if a given framework doesn't explicitly support MongoDB, don't view this as incompatibility. In a discussion with Paul Jones, the author of the Solar framework (and a fan of MongoDB), I asked him if they had plans to support MongoDB. His answer (parahprased): "Why? The driver does so much that I don't think we could add to it to make the experience any better." He's not alone; I know of a few other frameworks that have opted to stick with the driver without adding any additional support because it works so well.

The following frameworks have built support for MongoDB internally. Often it is not only to use it as a core data store, but to integrate it with additional components, such as as a backend for session handling.

Symfony2

Philosophically, Symfony2 believes you should be able to use what you want and provides a wonderful plugin architecture to permit you to do so. Sensio Labs, the parent of the Symfony project, also sponsors the Doctrine project and the two teams have a decent amount of overlap. Doctrine2 works quite well with Symfony2, providing both RDBMS and MongoDB support.

Lithium

Lithium is the first framework to boast support for NoSQL solutions right out of the box. In fact, originally it only supported MongoDB and CouchDB. The Lithium project was started by Nate Abele, the former lead developer of the CakePHP framework.

Zend

Zend, the PHP company, has been developing its own framework for a few years. It is widely used, and through the Shanty Mongo plugin, has MongoDB support. Shanty Mongo is an ODM like many of the libraries mentioned here. There is currently a proposal for MongoDB to have full support for an upcoming release of Zend Framework. Additionally, a number of components will support MongoDB in upcoming releases.

Fuel

Fuel supports MongoDB out of the box. It provides a simple wrapper that isn't any simpler than the driver.

FatFree Framework

The FatFree Framework—or F3, as it's commonly called—provides M2, the Mongo Mapper library, to interface with MongoDB.

CHAPTER 5
Conclusion

Thanks for sticking with me through these pages. I've endeavored to not only inform and instruct, but also to give you insight into the future of software development. I first encountered MongoDB in the spring of 2010. I was the new head of engineering at OpenSky, a social ecommerce company in New York City. Their existing infrastructure was crippled by the weight of their growth, and it was clear that a better solution was needed. As we began to plan out a restructure of the application, we put all possibilities on the table. Initially, we decided to build OpenSky using PHP (with the Symfony2 framework) and MySQL. At the time, I felt that none of the NoSQL solutions were ready for production use, but one technology in particular piqued my interest and I decided we would use it to power an auxiliary component to the application. We first used MongoDB for logging. Within a couple of weeks of using it, I had a huge epiphany. I was amazed by the potential it brought. It had the potential to radically alter the way we built software, not just at OpenSky, but for the industry as a whole. I saw MongoDB as that once-in-a-decade (or two) technology that is so disruptive that it changes everything. We very quickly threw away all that we were doing with MySQL and switched over completely to MongoDB for our entire application. Our product launched ahead of an aggressive schedule and never once struggled to keep up with the explosive growth OpenSky experienced. I can easily look back on that decision as one of the best I have made in my career.

For our team, MongoDB didn't represent just a database, but an enabler. It enabled us to do truly rapid and agile development. We no longer needed to spend the first third of an iteration planning out our database schema with rigid precision (only to not get it perfect and spend the next third of the iteration writing alter statements and conversion scripts). We were enabled to build a great product without worrying about all the complications of SQL and caching. Imagine how much time you have spent wrestling with databases, caching layers and making sure to expire all the right data; debugging complex queries with loads of joins or learning a new interface as each new ORM came out. All the time you have spent dealing with security challenges of sanitizing everything to prevent SQL injection attacks. All the schema migration scripts you've written. What if you took that time and instead focused on building the best application you know how? For me, MongoDB has become more than just a database and is rather a tool that's enabled me to do what I love most: write great code.

My hope is that you have been able to feel a bit of this as you read this book. Now go out and build something great!

About the Author

Steve Francia, Chief Solutions Architect at 10gen, is responsible for all language drivers, integrations, evangelism, web, and docs. Prior to 10gen, Steve led OpenSky to become the first ecommerce site powered by MongoDB and one of the first PHP sites backed by MongoDB. His previous roles include CIO/COO at Portero, VP of Development at Takkle, and founder and CTO of Supernerd. Steve loves open source. He has contributed to dozens of open source projects, including MongoDB, Doctrine, Symfony2, Magento, and Zoop and has started a few of his own. Steve is a frequent speaker at conferences around the world on databases, e-commerce, big data, and application development. He also maintains an active blog at *http://www.spf13.com*. Steve holds a BA from Brigham Young University, where—among other things—he created and taught a course on dynamic web development.

Get even more for your money.

Join the O'Reilly Community, and register the O'Reilly books you own. It's free, and you'll get:

- $4.99 ebook upgrade offer
- 40% upgrade offer on O'Reilly print books
- Membership discounts on books and events
- Free lifetime updates to ebooks and videos
- Multiple ebook formats, DRM FREE
- Participation in the O'Reilly community
- Newsletters
- Account management
- 100% Satisfaction Guarantee

Signing up is easy:

1. **Go to: oreilly.com/go/register**
2. **Create an O'Reilly login.**
3. **Provide your address.**
4. **Register your books.**

Note: English-language books only

To order books online:
oreilly.com/store

For questions about products or an order:
orders@oreilly.com

To sign up to get topic-specific email announcements and/or news about upcoming books, conferences, special offers, and new technologies:
elists@oreilly.com

For technical questions about book content:
booktech@oreilly.com

To submit new book proposals to our editors:
proposals@oreilly.com

O'Reilly books are available in multiple DRM-free ebook formats. For more information:
oreilly.com/ebooks

Spreading the knowledge of innovators   oreilly.com

The information you need, when and where you need it.

With Safari Books Online, you can:

Access the contents of thousands of technology and business books

- Quickly search over 7000 books and certification guides
- Download whole books or chapters in PDF format, at no extra cost, to print or read on the go
- Copy and paste code
- Save up to 35% on O'Reilly print books
- **New!** Access mobile-friendly books directly from cell phones and mobile devices

Stay up-to-date on emerging topics before the books are published

- Get on-demand access to evolving manuscripts.
- Interact directly with authors of upcoming books

Explore thousands of hours of video on technology and design topics

- Learn from expert video tutorials
- Watch and replay recorded conference sessions

Lightning Source UK Ltd.
Milton Keynes UK
UKOW020012120912

198845UK00003B/24/P

9 781449 314361